LOST AND FOUND

A Children's Christmas Play

BY

KATHLEEN MORRIS

Rouge Publishing

OTHER BOOKS BY KATHLEEN MORRIS

<u>Deep Bay Series</u>
Deep Bay Vengeance
Deep Bay Relic
Deep Bay Legacy (Coming 2014)
<u>Blood War Series</u>
The Prion Attachment
Blood Purge (Coming 2014)
<u>Short Inspirations Series</u>
Size Seven Shorts
Short End Of The Stick
Shortcut To Alaska
<u>Short Stories</u>
Along The Way - 12 Short Stories You Can
Read Along The Way
<u>Plays</u>
Time Will Tell - An Easter Play
Even Me - A Christmas Play For Your
Sunday School
All I Need Is Love - A Play For Teens
Lost And Found - A Children's Christmas
Play
Gotta Love It - A Humorous Play About
Rural Life

How - To Books
How To Make Eye Catching Ebook Covers Easily

Available on Amazon.com

Table of Contents

A NOTE FROM THE AUTHOR

This play was originally performed in Arlee, Saskatchewan, Canada, for a children's Christmas Sunday School program in December 2003. It was originally done as a musical and can have many current Christmas carols incorporated into it. It is my desire to keep Christ in Christmas and to lead others to Him through my writing so that we who are lost, can surely be found again, through the loving hope of Jesus Christ.

DEDICATION

This play is dedicated to all my lovely friends from the Arlee Church. You my friends, are one of a kind. Your love and generosity inspired me to write this because it was that love, that reflected Jesus through everything you did. I would also like to dedicate this play to my three children, Renee, Philip, and Brett, because the memories came flooding back to me as I envisioned you as little ones, dressed in costume, performing this play way back when. May your hearts always follow Christ no matter what! And if you ever need to find your way back to Him...remember this play. He will always find his sheep!

CHARACTERS

Narrator:
Narrates the entire play and brings the story together.

John:
The oldest of three shepherd brothers.

Peter:
The second oldest of three shepherd brothers.

Thomas:
The youngest of three shepherd brothers.

Angel:

Messenger Angel – tells everyone about the birth of Christ.

Miscellaneous Angels:

A group of kids dressed as Angels.

Mary:

Plays the part of mother Mary and also sings a solo.

Joseph:

Plays the part of Joseph, Mary's fiancé.

Miscellaneous sheep:

They have no speaking parts, they only make the sound of sheep. This part can be played by young children dressed up in sheep costumes.

SCENE ONE

The stage is decorated like a field, or a hill. It will be the backdrop for the entire play, whereby a second manger scene will be added later. It is really up to you on how you want to decorate. Christmas decorations can even be used such as a star, lights, etc.

Narrator:
It was an incredible night. The stars peppered the twilight sky as they marked the pathway to something beautiful, something bright, and more brilliant than the sun or the moon. Yes, this night, the shepherds seem to be drawn to it. (*Shepherds enter*) On the hill overlooking Bethlehem, three shepherds

gazed at the luminous heavens with amazement. They wandered far from the flock they were supposed to be watching, when suddenly John, the oldest, realized the sheep were missing.

John:
Where are the sheep? You guys... Peter! Thomas! (*John shakes the two shepherds until they finally take their eyes off the sky*) Where are the sheep?

Peter:
(*Looking around*) Uh...oh! Dad's going to kill us.

Thomas:
You were supposed to stay with them Peter.

Peter:
Was not! (*They both start fighting*)

John:
Stop it you guys. We're not going to find them like that.

Narrator:

So the three shepherds set off to find the lost sheep. It wasn't an easy task considering they couldn't keep their eyes off the glowing star over Bethlehem. Yet, distracted as they were, they managed to focus on the task at hand. They looked far, they looked low, they even looked in the most unusual places. (*Shepherds act as if they are looking everywhere possible*) But no sheep could be found. Will their flock be lost forever? Could wee little vulnerable sheep survive on their own out in this frightful desert? Questions filled their heads as they talked amongst themselves. Could the sheep have followed the star as they themselves had so desperately wanted to do? John, Peter, and Thomas, began to look to the sky again. The star was glowing brighter now. It seemed to be moving toward them. They huddled together in fright.

Angel:

Don't be afraid. I bring you good news of great joy that will be for all the people. Today in the town of David, a Saviour has been born to you; He is Christ the Lord. This will be a sign to you: You will find a baby wrapped in cloths and lying in a manger.

Narrator:
Suddenly a great company of heavenly hosts appeared with the angel, praising God and saying:

All Angels:
Glory to God in the highest, and on earth, peace to men on whom his favour rests. (*Angels Sing song here. They can choose "Angels we have heard on high" or any other suitable carol. It is left up to you*)

(*Angels exit*)

Narrator:
Later, the three shepherd's decided they had better get over to Bethlehem. They knew they still needed to find their sheep, but if the Angels told him to go, then they must do it. As for the lost sheep, all three of them

blamed themselves. They knew the sheep were in danger if they had already entered the big city.

John:
(*He hangs his head down*) The sheep were my responsibility. If it wasn't for me, they would be safe now.

Peter:
No John, it's my fault. I should have listened to you. If I would have stayed back to protect them like I was told to, they wouldn't be lost.

Thomas:
No, you guys, it's my fault. I saw them running away, and I did nothing.

Narrator:
So, discouraged because they could not find their sheep, yet excited because they were going to see the King, they set out on their difficult journey to Bethlehem. (*Shepherds exit stage*) Congregation, will you please rise and sing, "Oh Little Town Of Bethlehem".

(After the song, the narrator tells them to sit) You may be seated.

SCENE TWO

(At this point the manger scene is brought out)

Narrator:

In the busy town of Bethlehem, the night air reddened Mary's cheeks as she rocked her baby. She had never seen a child so beautiful. It was hard to imagine he was her own. Yet, to her, he did not belong. This child, this baby in her arms, belongs to everyone. She would have to force herself to accept it though she didn't want to. But, she couldn't fight the truth. He was what the angel had promised. And now, this day, this redeeming day, she looked into her child's cherub face and sang him a forever lullaby.

Mary:

(Sing solo – either, "Silent Night" or any other appropriate carol)

Narrator:

To Mary, this child was a gift. She truly had been blessed. Yet, with all the visitors she had lately, she couldn't help but feel a bit tired. She laid Jesus down in the manger and decided to take a nap.

(Joseph enters)

Joseph:

Oh, sorry Mary, I didn't know you were trying to sleep.

Mary:

That's okay Joseph. I wasn't sleeping yet.

Joseph:

You want me to watch the baby for a while?

Mary:

No…he'll be okay. I just want to take a quick nap. Maybe you could go to the market though. I'm sooo hungry.

Joseph:

Yah, me too. I'll see what I can find. (*Joseph exits*)

Mary:

(*Yawning, and leaning against something, she talks to the baby*) You are such a sweetheart…yes you are. Mommy's little man…but then you know you're something much more than that...yes you do. (*Mary nods off to sleep*)

Narrator:

As Mary silently sleeps, she dreams of Jesus. He is grown now and preaching in the synagogue. He is also sleeping calmly in a boat fishing with other men during a storm. Then she sees him as a great leader. At one point, he even feeds five thousand people. She watches him turn water into wine. He can even walk on water. Yes, Mary smiled at the wonders of God's only son. On one occasion, Mary sees something in her dream that puzzles her. Suddenly, her heart begins to ache. She sees a crown of thorns, a cross, a blackened sinful day…a heckling crowd that now hates her precious little Jesus. No…she didn't want to see. She wouldn't believe this… No! She tossed and turned in her sleep until peace came over her. This piece illuminated her dream until she realized that the truth would set her free from this nightmare. Yes, the truth would set everyone free.

Suddenly, with a start, Mary woke from her sleep. She wiped the tears from her eyes as she noticed the many sheep running up to her. (*All the sheep enter*) They kept their distance, but she wondered where they had come from, and who was taking care of them.

All sheep:
Baaa Baaa Baaa (*They parade around Mary and the baby and then sit down around her*)

Mary:

Well, hello there little sheep…and where is your shepherd? Or did you come to see my baby too?

(*Shepherds enter the stage with Mary and sheep*)

John:

There they are you guys! (*John points to the sheep*)

Peter:

The sheep! The sheep! We found them! (*All three bow*) Is this the Messiah the angel told us about?

Mary:

Yes gentlemen it is.

Thomas:

This is for Him. (*He takes one of the sheep by the hand and leads it over to Mary and the baby*) This lamb is the finest we have.

Peter:

Yes, you see, we lost our sheep a while ago, but now they're found. Thank you! Thank you so much!

Mary:

I didn't find them…but thank you for the gift anyway. Jesus will love it.

Narrator:

The three shepherds were overwhelmed to see the Messiah that day. They played with him and tickled him. They held him and admired him. (*Shepherds hold the baby and play with him*) They stayed most of the day and remembered it well. For on this day, the world changed forever. As for the sheep, the shepherds never knew who found their flock for them, but we do. We know who finds the lost. We know who heals the broken-hearted and sets the captives free. We know who looks after us when we lose our way. Jesus was born so that we may have light to see. He was born that we might be found. If you are lost this Christmas season – If you can't find your way back home –If you put your faith in other people, or in your possessions, know that these things cannot save you when you walk amongst a big dark city like Bethlehem, or even a small town like_____(*put the name of your own town/city/community here and adjust accordingly*) Only Jesus can find you! Let him be your shepherd today.

(*Cast and crew stand and sing a Christmas Carol. You can choose any that may suit*)

(*Ending Song*)

(*After the song is finished, all join hands on stage and bow*)

Narrator:
Congregation...please rise and sing, "Joy To The World" with us.

THE END

ABOUT THE AUTHOR

Award-winning author Kathleen Morris has written numerous articles, poetry, and short stories published in various Saskatchewan newspapers. Her poem *Refuge* is published in a book anthology titled *A Golden Morning*. She has written many plays and skits including her play titled *Gotta Love It*, winner of Dancing Sky Theatre's rural writing contest in 2001 where it was also performed by the theatre troupe in Meacham, Saskatchewan.

Deep Bay Vengeance is Kathleen's first novel followed by its sequel *Deep Bay Relic*. She also writes non-fiction inspirational books about funny stories from her own life. Her latest novel is called *The Prion Attachment,* first book in the *Blood War Trilogy.* When she's not writing, she enjoys spending time with her husband Barry and their three grown children at her home in Saskatchewan, Canada. For more on Kathleen Morris please check out her Amazon Author page at Amazon.com

OTHER BOOKS BY KATHLEEN MORRIS

<u>Deep Bay Series</u>
Deep Bay Vengeance
Deep Bay Relic
Deep Bay Legacy (Coming 2014)
<u>Blood War Series</u>
The Prion Attachment
Blood Purge (Coming 2014)
<u>Short Inspirations Series</u>
Size Seven Shorts
Short End Of The Stick
Shortcut To Alaska
<u>Short Stories</u>
Along The Way - 12 Short Stories You Can
Read Along The Way
<u>Plays</u>
Time Will Tell - An Easter Play
Even Me - A Christmas Play For Your
Sunday School
All I Need Is Love - A Play For Teens
Lost And Found - A Children's Christmas
Play
Gotta Love It - A Humorous Play About
Rural Life

<u>How - To Books</u>
How To Make Eye Catching Ebook Covers
Easily

Available on Amazon.com

www.ingramcontent.com/pod-product-compliance
Lightning Source LLC
LaVergne TN
LVHW051819080426
835513LV00017B/2017